Tears
and
Tossings

Tears *and* Tossings

Hope *in* the Waves *of* Life

Sarah Walton

10 Publishing
a division of 10ofthose.com

Unless otherwise stated, Scripture quotations are from The Holy Bible, New International Version ®, NIV ®. Copyright © 1973, 1978, 1984, 2011 by Biblica, Inc. ® Used by permission. All rights reserved worldwide.

Scripture quotations marked ESV are from The Holy Bible, English Standard Version ESV ®. Copyright © 2001 by Crossway Bibles, a publishing ministry of Good News Publishers. Used by permission. All rights reserved.

Copyright © 2022 by Sarah Walton

First published in Great Britain in 2022

The right of Sarah Walton to be identified as the Author of this Work has been asserted by her in accordance with the Copyright, Designs and Patents Act 1988.

All rights reserved. No part of this publication may be reproduced, stored in a retrieval system or transmitted in any form or by any means, electronic, mechanical, photocopying, recording or otherwise, without the prior permission of the publisher or the Copyright Licensing Agency.

British Library Cataloguing in Publication Data
A record for this book is available from the British Library

ISBN: 978-1-914966-18-7

Designed by Jude May

Cover image © Ekaterina Romanova, iStock
Printed in Denmark by Nørhaven

10Publishing, a division of 10ofthose.com
Unit C, Tomlinson Road, Leyland, PR25 2DY, England
Email: info@10ofthose.com
Website: www.10ofthose.com

1 3 5 7 10 8 6 4 2

Contents

I

When suffering strikes

I stirred uncomfortably in my seat, struggling to accept the reality that this chair had my name on it for a reason. I sat there quietly and listened as the group went around sharing their personal journey of sorrow, loss, and grief. Each person represented a unique story, with their own circumstances, experiences, personalities, cultures, and beliefs. But we all shared one thing in common—the heartache of a life we never expected. Regardless of how different we were, we knew pain and all the outworkings of its unwanted presence.

As we shared, one thing was clear—we were all searching for comfort, purpose, hope, and healing in our pain. There were no simple fixes or empty platitudes that would bring comfort to the agony of those who'd lost a child, were raising a child with life-altering needs, reeling from rejection or abuse, battling a cancer diagnosis, or struggling to put food on the table for their family. No matter how we try to sugarcoat it or find a silver lining, there's something about suffering and loss that shakes our confidence, disorients us, dulls the things we once enjoyed, and brings questions that demand an answer.

Why me? we wonder. *What's the purpose of my suffering? Do my tears just fall to the ground as useless? If my pain is for nothing, then what hope do I have within it? If this life is all there is, what's the point? Or, is it possible that my tears point me to something or someone greater? If there is a God, does he see and care about me personally? And if he does, why is he allowing this pain if he really loves me?*

If you've asked these questions, I'm right there with you. Although I have a lot to be grateful for, much of my life has been filled with various forms of pain, sorrow, and loss. Loneliness has been a frequent visitor, grief is often just under the surface, and, at times, tears have been the only language I've known how to speak.

My story

I grew up with loving parents and had a fairly uneventful childhood, but it was also marked from very early on with pain. As a child, I faced ongoing physical ailments which no one seemed able to explain or solve. My teen years brought an abrupt end to my joy of athletics, coupled with sexual abuse from classmates and increasing health challenges. My life unraveled before me, landing me in a pit so dark and deep that there was no foreseeable way out. At the age of seventeen, I found myself in the adolescent psychiatric ward of a hospital.

If there's such a thing as "hitting rock bottom," I had reached it.

I was lost. I was deeply hurting. And I desperately needed something—or Someone—to give me a reason to go on. Thankfully, the trajectory of my life was forever changed in that hospital room—a trajectory that would be far from easy, but one that gave me a hope and purpose to go on.

Fast forward three years and, much to my own surprise, I met my husband (Jeff) and we were married shortly after I turned twenty. Although this wasn't the path I expected to be on, we were excited to embark on our life together. Three years later, we welcomed our first child into the world and were filled with hopes and dreams for our growing family. But those came to a screeching halt as we rushed our seven-week-old baby to the emergency room with a high fever and words from the doctor that no parent ever wants to hear: "We don't know what's wrong, but it doesn't look good." For five long days and nights we waited, with no answers and growing concern in the doctors' faces. Although nothing was found other than evidence of an "unknown severe infection," the heavy doses of medicine finally took effect. After many sleepless nights and countless prayers, we were sent home with overwhelming gratitude that we were leaving with the child we had been prepared to go home without.

Little did we know that what happened to him in those five days would affect him (and our whole family) for years to come—possibly a lifetime. Frequent sickness, weight loss, increasingly difficult behaviors, uncontrollable and long-lasting tantrums, unreasonable responses to normal situations, neurological and physical struggles that no doctor could give answers to, and overwhelming stress in our home led to a life of mere survival. Our son was bright, sweet, and funny at times, but his illness impacted every aspect of our lives. The hours seemed like days, and the days seemed like years. Before we knew it, six long years had gone by and our family of three gradually grew to a family of six.

During this time, Jeff worked long hours, on call twenty-four hours a day, seven days a week as an orthopedic trauma consultant. It provided a comfortable salary, but made for a very uncomfortable family life. Over time, my health drastically declined, the challenges of our child's behavioral and neurological outbursts increased, and our other three children began to complain of their own aches and pains. Our family was in crisis.

In a drastic step to save our family, Jeff took nearly a seventy percent pay cut in order to change jobs and be more available to help with our declining home life. It took immense sacrifice to walk away from a comfortable salary, sell the home we loved, and downsize to a rental home, but it seemed clear that the cost would be worth it in the long run. However, a year later, Jeff was caught up in company-wide cutbacks and was left without a job. Once the shock wore off, anger, questions, confusion, and tears were frequent visitors. With chronic health issues, special-needs challenges, the loss of our beautiful home, no income, and us living off food stamps, it seemed like things couldn't possibly get worse.

Until they did.

In 2015, I was finally led to doctors who were able to connect all of my various health issues to years of untreated Lyme disease and other related autoimmune issues. Over the following year, as each of our children's aches and pains increased, tests revealed that my active Lyme infection had been passed on to all four of them in pregnancy. I was a mom battling a chronic, difficult-to-treat infection, while carrying the grief, guilt, and burden of knowing that I had brought four children into the world who now suffered from the very same disease. On top of it all, we had no income to pay for the out-of-pocket costs for treatments. Honestly, it felt like more than I could bear.

The sorrows weighed heavily and the tears came often. They came when I watched my children suffer things that I felt helpless to change. They flowed when the pain in my body made it feel like I was watching life happen, rather than living it. They came as my husband and I worked through the painful trials that put increasing strain on our marriage. They flowed as I endured my fifth ankle surgery and was told I would increasingly lose my ability to walk. They came when I feared the future would be more than I could bear. They came when Jeff was swept up in a second company-wide layoff three months after he was hired. And the tears still flow every time I watch my son suffer from something that no child (or adult) should ever have to endure.

There's no denying that I have carried a weight of sorrows I never thought possible and shed tears to the point where there have been no tears left to shed. Pain and heartache have caused me to ask difficult questions and search for their answers, desperate for a hope and purpose in all this pain.

My guess is, if you're picking up this book, you are too.

Maybe you're carrying some form of sorrow and know what it's like to shed tears over loss, disappointment, heartache, or physical, emotional, or mental pain. If that's you, I'm so very sorry. Maybe you've always felt in control of your life but now circumstances have left you disoriented and shaken. Or maybe you've endured long and layered suffering, and you're wondering if there's any point in getting out of bed each morning.

Maybe you've searched for answers, but still feel like something is missing. Or maybe you've heard about the God of the Bible, but you're struggling to understand why a "good God" would allow you to suffer.

Well, friend, you're not alone. I'm still in the trenches of my suffering with no end in sight, and I certainly don't have all the answers. But I'm learning that there's Someone who does, and it's changed everything for me. It hasn't removed my suffering, but I've found a strength, hope, peace, and joy that my circumstances haven't been able to diminish. I'm learning that the God of the Bible is not a distant, uncaring God, but he's a compassionate, merciful, loving Father who sees us at our worst and still wants to come near to us, comfort us, and provide what we need. He's a God who has compassion toward our frailty and weaknesses, and grieves with us in our grief and sorrow. And he's a God who sees our tears when no one else does. As the Bible says in Psalm 56:8–9,

You have kept count of my tossings;
  put my tears in your bottle.
  Are they not in your book?
. . . This I know, that God is for me (ESV).

This doesn't lessen the pain of my circumstances or make life easier. Yet it tells me that somehow my pain isn't pointless, and there's a God who loves me, knows me, and not only sees my sorrows and tears, but holds them as if they are his own.

No matter what you're facing right now, what's happened in the past, what questions you have, or what you do or don't understand about God, the same can be true of you. You don't have to put your struggles, fears, sorrows, and tears aside. Just come as you are, with whatever griefs you bear, guilt you carry, insecurities you feel, or tears that may fall.

Friend, could it be that there's more to our pain than meets the eye? Could it be that our tears are not only seen but held by God himself? If not, then our pain in this life is nothing more than something to endure. But if this is true, and God is good, loving, and compassionate, then there's comfort to be found in knowing that our sufferings are not pointless or hopeless.

Pain is real. But so is hope.

2

He holds our tears
in loneliness

At a moment's notice, chaos can erupt in my home. This day was no different.

Although every day is difficult with my son's illness, some stand out as ones that will forever be etched in my mind. And this was one of them.

Something triggered him, as had happened countless times before, and a two-hour-long episode began. As chaos went on around me and he suffered at the hands of his illness, my adrenaline pumped within me and I leapt into action, buckling down for the long haul. By the time it had passed, he had melted into my arms in tears, and I was left with an aching heart and an exhausted body.

But worst of all, I was enveloped in an overwhelming sense of loneliness.

Not only was I physically alone, but the longer our son's challenges lasted, the more isolating it became. Very few could relate to our specific circumstances and most barely knew they existed. Even countless doctors were at a loss as to the cause, let alone the solution. As the years have gone by and the challenges have increased over the past decade, the loneliness has grown exponentially.

I now sat on the floor, holding back tears as the other kids chased each other around the house, blissfully unaware of all that had just transpired. Even with noise all around me, the loneliness grew louder.

A knock at the door interrupted my runaway thoughts. I gathered myself and opened it to find on my doorstep a small box containing a small, clear bottle. No note, no signature, just a little bottle with a tiny scroll rolled up inside.

I slowly unrolled the fragile piece of paper and read these words:

You have kept count of my tossings;
*   put my tears in your bottle.*

Are they not in your book?
. . . This I know, that God is for me.[1]

I stood there for a moment, still perplexed by the unexplained box on my doorstep with no one in sight. But a small wave of comfort began to wash over me. In this moment of incredible heartache that no one could see but me, I felt seen and, somehow, less alone.

Is God really for me? I wondered. Does he really keep track of every sorrow that causes me to toss in bed at night and every tear that falls when no one else can see? As I thought back to all that I had endured over the years and all that still loomed in front of me, these few words carried so much weight. To be seen and known—we all desire that, don't we?

And yet, when grief or pain take up residence in our lives, we often feel unseen and unknown as the life we knew comes to a halt and life around us goes on as usual. We can walk into a bustling group and feel lonelier than when we're alone.

Loneliness comes in all shapes and forms. At times, physical illness or a special-needs child prevent us from typical life activities, forcing us into isolation. At other times, we experience a loss or trial to which very few relate. Even if they've experienced something similar, our different personalities, temperaments, and unique aspects still create a feeling of loneliness. Sometimes, we may act like the life of the party on the outside, but feel utterly alone on the inside—and we may not even know why.

For me, loneliness has come and gone in intensity, but the nature of our circumstances has often forced me into some level of isolation. Even when I'm with others, there is a large part of my life that I'm unable to share due to the complexity of our situation. If I try to explain, I'm often met with blank stares and awkward silence.

Relationship and community are important and we need to pursue them as much as possible. However, if you've dealt with true loneliness, you know that sometimes that's easier said than done.

But what if there is Someone who sees and knows us like no one else ever could? Could it be that there's a God who wants to draw near in the messiness of our grief and loneliness, unlike those who shrink back in discomfort? Could it be that he sees us in the dark of night when painful and anxious thoughts rob us of sleep? Could it be that he sees the tears that come when no one else is watching? And if so, could it be that those tears, and the circumstances that provoke them, truly matter to him?

A God of seeing

Thankfully, there's an account in the Bible, which is God's words to humankind, that began to answer this question for me. Chapter 16 of Genesis, the first book of the Bible, tells of a servant girl, Hagar, who was unfairly treated for someone else's gain, and eventually forced to flee into the wilderness for the safety of herself and her young child. Alone in the wilderness, she not only felt rejected and uncared for, but was faced with the imminent threat of them both dying at the hands of the harsh wilderness. Can you imagine how despairing and alone she must have felt?

However, right when things must have seemed hopeless, an angel of the Lord found her. In the middle of the vast wilderness, where no one else could see her, God saw the outcast, hurting, tear-streaked face of Hagar and he came to her. So she called him *"a God of seeing,"*[2] because he saw her and looked after her when no one else could or would.

If God saw Hagar in the wilderness when no one else could, surely he sees you and me in the wilderness of our own painful circumstances. Not only does he see our tears, but he is able and willing to comfort us in ways that no one else can. He can carry us in our sorrows.

A friend who sticks closer than a brother

As I've had to learn the hard way, no matter how much I want to feel seen and heard by family and friends, there's only so much they can understand and so much they can endure. The longer our suffering lasts, those willing to stick with us become few and far between.

But the Bible says that *"there is a friend who sticks closer than a brother."*[3] Even if everyone else abandons us or can't see and understand our pain, there is a friend, Jesus, who promises to never leave or forsake those who put their trust in him. As the Bible also states, *"The LORD himself goes before you and will be with you; he will never leave you nor forsake you. Do not be afraid; do not be discouraged."*[4]

Friend, whether you know it or believe it right now, God sees you personally. He knows your deepest fears, greatest desires, and heaviest heartache. You may be carrying sorrows and burdens that no one else can see or carry at the moment, but be comforted to know that Jesus loves you so much that he gave his life for you and wants to come near to you with compassion.

And he not only sees you, but he came to give you a hope that loneliness cannot steal. When we trust Jesus as our Savior, he promises our lonely tears are held by God himself.

Never alone

Whenever I glance over at that little bottle sitting by my kitchen sink, I'm grateful it showed up at my door. To most people, it probably looks like nothing more than a strange choice of decoration. To me, though, this little bottle carries far more meaning than anything it could physically hold.

Whatever tomorrow may hold, that bottle will forever be a reminder that the God of the Bible knows and profoundly loves me (and you). Out of a world full of people, he personally sees and comes close to us in our loneliness. He is strong enough to hold what you and I cannot. If you trust him, he will draw near to you and fill you with a hope and comfort that cannot be taken.

You may not feel seen by those around you, but with Jesus, you're never truly alone.

3

He holds our tears in grief and loss

Disoriented. Numb. Somber. There are few words to describe where my heart has been lately. I've found myself in a place of weariness where I've rarely been before. Maybe it's a physical response of survival, or maybe it's an escape mechanism. Either way, I've found myself detached, struggling to find my way out of the darkness and heaviness of grief. I have always been a fighter, for better or worse. But it's a scary place when you feel your fight begin to fade.

As the losses continue to grow, grief has dulled the joys of life, robbed me of sleep, and caused my body to pay the price.

Our losses have come in many shapes and sizes. Some are larger (such as my health, our kids' health, our son's special needs, my degenerative ankle, and the death of loved ones). Others are smaller (such as of a job, a comfortable bank account, the home we loved, and the family life we expected).

But whatever the nature or intensity of loss may be, grief is never far behind.

Where do we go from here?

Let yourself grieve

When loss strikes, I tend to respond in one of two ways. I either stuff my emotions down, doing all I can to distract myself from reality, or I face the pain head on and let myself grieve what's been lost. At face value, we see grief as a sign of weakness. I believe the contrary: that grief shows courage. It says, "This loss hurts and instead of running from it, I'm going to acknowledge it and grieve what I've lost."

In essence, our grief simply acknowledges that things aren't as they should be.

So I can grieve the pain of my son's challenges every time I'm faced with a fresh reminder of what's been lost because of them. I can acknowledge my grief when I can't run around with my kids, exercise, or do many of the activities I once enjoyed—in order to preserve my ability to walk as long as possible. I can grieve when we have to change plans yet again as my chronic illness flares up. And I can grieve when my children look up at me with tears and ask why they have to struggle when they just want to be "normal" like kids around them.

There's no doubt these things are losses. They hurt. They remind me often that things aren't as they should be. And they make me long for something more.

Have you ever felt that way? Are you hurting from the loss of someone close to you? Are you struggling with the loss of your health, a friendship, or a job? Or are you struggling with the loss of a dream or opportunity, grappling with the loss of the life you expected?

If so, let yourself grieve it. It's right and good to acknowledge what's been lost or what may never be.

Grieve with hope

I admit, however, that simply acknowledging what's been lost and letting myself feel the pain of it doesn't actually bring me genuine comfort. It might help me process reality and give my body the ability to work through the shock, stress, anxiety, anger, and sorrow that often comes with these losses. If I have no hope beyond my grief, though, then it falls short of any real comfort.

But grief doesn't only acknowledge my pain; it's meant to point me—and you—to something greater: a better world where pain, loss, heartache, and death will one day be no more.

If this life is all there is, these painful losses are nothing more than pointless pain. But if there is a God who came to rescue us and bring us to a better home beyond this one, then these losses are only temporary.

This is the hope you and I can have even as we grieve what we've lost. Only those who turn to Jesus for their hope will experience this peace. Thankfully, though, Jesus explained how and where this hope is found.

As we read in the Bible, Jesus (who was the Son of God) said,

> *Do not let your hearts be troubled. You believe in God; believe also in me. My Father's house has many rooms; if that were not so, would I have*

told you that I am going there to prepare a place for you? And if I go and prepare a place for you, I will come back and take you to be with me that you also may be where I am. You know the way to the place where I am going.[5]

Jesus was talking here about heaven. This is not a boring place with floating angels in the clouds; it's a new and perfect heaven and earth that will one day be a reality for all who put their trust in Jesus. This future home will be perfect, painless, and filled with more pleasures than you and I could ever imagine. More than anything, we will live and walk with God himself.

Jesus also told us how we can have this hope. He said, *"I am the way and the truth and the life. No one comes to the Father except through me. If you really know me, you will know my Father as well."*[6] The Bible is clear that all people are sinners, that is we have all rejected God. As a result, we rightly deserve his punishment for our rebellion. But the incredible news is that we can be forgiven and accepted by God through trusting in his Son Jesus to save us from our sins and give us eternal life with him. There is no other way in which we can be saved and enjoy eternity in heaven.

Does that mean we'll no longer feel the pain of our losses in this world? No. Will we still grieve for now? Yes. But when we know that our suffering won't last forever and that there's something better beyond it, it gives us a reason to hope and persevere—even when it hurts.

I am confident that my precious son will one day be freed from all that torments his mind and body, and that he will finally experience the joy of being made whole. Though the days are hard and the future is unknown, knowing that he will one day be healed gives me the comfort and strength to endure through these darkest times. It also gives me the privilege of pointing him to this hope as I experience it in my own life.

Do you have this hope in your grief? If not, I encourage you—I implore you—not to wait to find it. Bring your grief to the God who created you and loves you, and receive the hope and comfort he offers you through Jesus.

Don't grieve alone

When I'm hurting, it's not easy to let in others. I rarely feel comfortable showing my vulnerability in front of others, especially when those around me seem to have it all together. Even though it can be good to let a few safe people into our grieving process, no one will ever fully know the depths of our sorrows—except God himself.

And here's the thing—we don't have to grieve alone. There's a God who feels our pain and grieves with us in it. He's not far off or unable to comfort us and provide what we need; he's a God of mercy and a perfect Father who promises to come near and comfort us in all our pain and suffering.

Believe it or not, the Bible isn't just a set of rules. It's God's life-giving words to us, which apply to all aspects of our life—including our losses and grief. One writer in the Bible shows us that we can cry out to God in raw honesty, saying, *"Be merciful to me, LORD, for I am in distress; my eyes grow weak with sorrow, my soul and body with grief. My life is consumed by anguish and my years by groaning; my strength fails because of my affliction, and my bones grow weak."*[7] I don't know about you, but I can relate to those words. All throughout history, men and women who have believed the words of God have also known that they could be completely honest with him, even in the messiness of their grief.

In fact, the Bible even calls Jesus "a man of sorrows."[8] He left the comforts of heaven to come to earth as a human, knowing that he would suffer pain, temptations, loss, fears, grief, and a horrific death on a cross. Because of his relentless love for us, Jesus died in our place, taking not only the punishment our sins against God deserve, but all of the griefs and sorrows we experience in this world as a result. Jesus knows what it's like to carry a crushing weight that no one else can: *"he was pierced for our transgressions, he was crushed for our iniquities; the punishment that brought us peace was on him, and by his wounds we are healed."*[9]

Jesus *chose* to come to earth. Being God, he could have avoided the pain of this world and left us to ourselves. But he chose not to do that. He chose to come to earth and experience all that we experience—including loss, sorrow, struggle, inconvenience, disappointment, pain, grief, and loneliness. He knows the full extent of our sorrows and can empathize with and comfort us as Someone who's experienced them himself. Because Jesus knows what it's like to be rejected, laughed at, and misunderstood, he can empathize with us in our loneliness. Because he experienced physical pain, he can comfort us in ours. Because he faced the loss of loved ones, friendships, comforts, a place to call home, and life itself, he can understand our losses more than anyone ever will. And because he shed his own tears, he feels the weight of ours.

I'm so thankful that we don't have to have it all together or walk through our grief alone. We can tell our sorrows to God in honesty, and be comforted to know that he's been there.

Grief that won't be wasted

I admit, I'm grieving even as I write this. The painful losses of my life are far from over and I'm reminded daily of the grief that frequently comes as a result. Truthfully, if I didn't have hope beyond these losses, I'm not sure if I could endure another day.

But as I've grieved these losses, God has used them to show me that although they may be painful, they don't have to be pointless. They can lead us to the comfort, truth, and hope that Jesus came to earth to give us. A hope that gives us not only strength and comfort today, but purpose and hope for the eternal home he is preparing for those who put their trust in him.

Friend, it's okay to grieve your losses, but don't grieve them alone. Come to Jesus, the Man of Sorrows. You can trust him to not only forgive your sins, but to carry your griefs and give you hope in your losses.

With God, our tears do not fall unnoticed. He sees them, grieves them, and holds them as if they're his own.

4

He holds our tears
in hopelessness

"**M**om! Dad! Something keeps biting me!" one of our children yelled. We ran into the family room to investigate what was happening. As soon as I realized the cause, I froze. Fleas! Nope, no way, this was too much. Everything in me wanted to run for the hills, escape the horror we were living in, and never look back.

"I can't take it anymore!" I vented to Jeff a little while later. The layers of trials seemed too great. We had already experienced so much suffering: the life-altering challenges with our son were all-consuming; all four of our kids and I were growing weary from a daily battle with chronic illness; we had needed to walk away from our beautiful home and a comfortable salary due to the increasing challenges at home; we were facing overwhelming medical expenses; Jeff had unexpectedly lost the lower paid job to which he'd sacrificially switched; and I was slowly losing my ability to walk. And now our rental home was infested with fleas.

Life had been incredibly hard for years, but this latest trial felt like more than I could bear. To be honest, I felt utterly hopeless. I didn't want to live in my diseased and hurting body; I didn't want to live in the chaos of our special-needs challenges; and I certainly didn't want to live in a flea-infested home.

Everything in me wanted to escape, but I had nowhere to run.

A few days later, I picked up *The Hiding Place*, the biographical story of Corrie and Betsie ten Boom, who had risked their lives to hide countless Jews during World War Two until they were arrested and taken to a concentration camp. My own worries drifted into the background as I became engrossed in the horrors they were living.

At the point I had reached in the book, Betsie and Corrie had just been moved to a new barracks. The "beds" were nothing more than boards stacked on top of each other and the blankets were scarce, despite the freezing temperatures. Before long, they realized that this barrack was even worse than they imagined—it was infested with fleas!

My eyes widened. "Fleas?!" I nearly laughed out loud, not because there was anything funny about the horrors that they were enduring, but because of the pure irony in light of my current situation.

There had to be a reason for this coincidence.

As I kept reading, Betsie and Corrie had somehow managed to keep a Bible hidden as the guards would do their nightly rounds. After a few days, they noticed something strange was happening: the guards had stopped checking their barracks altogether. As time went on, Betsie and Corrie gained more confidence and began reading the Bible out loud to all the women who wanted to listen in their barracks. It became a lifeline for these suffering prisoners. Regardless of what they had previously believed about God, they soaked in the hope and comfort of the words they were hearing.

Night after night, they continued, until one day Betsie realized why the guards had stopped checking their barracks.

"You know we've never understood why we had so much freedom in the big room," she said. "Well—I found out."

That afternoon, she said, there'd been confusion in her knitting group about sock sizes and they'd asked the supervisor to come and settle it.

"But she wouldn't. She wouldn't even step through the door and neither would the guards. And you know why?"

Betsie could not keep from the triumph in her voice: "Because of the fleas! That's what she said, 'That place is crawling with fleas!'"

My mind rushed back to our first hour in this place. I remembered Betsie's bowed head, remembered her thanks to God for creatures I could see no use for.[10]

The words stopped me in my tracks: "her thanks to God for creatures I could see no use for." I sure couldn't see any use for any of our trials, let alone the fleas. But I felt a small flame of hope spark within me. If God could somehow take something as horrible as an infestation of fleas in a concentration camp and turn them into a blessing, surely he could bring something good out of my own, much less horrifying, circumstances. I realized at that moment how personal (and humorous!) God is to somehow bring good out of something as seemingly useless as fleas.

Even more, I felt seen and cared for, unable to deny that God had arranged for me to read this exact part of Corrie and Bestie's story at the time I most needed it. I was experiencing firsthand one of God's promises to us in the Bible: *"The LORD is close to the brokenhearted and saves those who are crushed in spirit."*[11]

Hope when circumstances appear hopeless

There are times in life when we face something incredibly difficult, but there are other times when we feel utterly hopeless. I admit, I've been there more times than I can count. However, it's also in these seasons when I've seen God's presence and tangible care for me most clearly.

Corrie ten Boom knew this. She goes on to explain in *The Hiding Place* about a time when the women in their barracks were getting sicker by the hour. She had a little medicine dropper of vitamins that she wanted to hoard, making sure she could save enough for her sister, Betsie, who was extremely ill. But as more women came to her, pleading for a drop of the medicine, she continued to sacrificially give a drop to each of them. After a while, they began to marvel at why this little bottle never seemed to run dry. Day after day, as woman after woman approached her, a drop would somehow always appear. Corrie tried to come up with some logical explanation, to which Betsie replied, *"Corrie, don't try too hard to explain it. Just accept it as a surprise from a Father who loves you."*[12]

One day, a delivery of vitamins surprisingly came to their barracks. When Corrie went to use up the old vitamin drops first, the bottle was completely empty. God hadn't taken away the reality of illness, but he had provided for them— in a way that showed them that he was not only a God of miracles, but was near and personally caring for their needs.

This has been true in my own life as well, often in moments when our circumstances have felt hopeless. During a season of job loss and when our needs were many, we started to pray asking God to provide what we needed. Then one morning, an unclaimed box of Christmas gifts anonymously showed up at our front door. To this day, we don't know from whom they came.

Another time, there was an unclaimed envelope of cash in our mailbox for the exact amount we needed for a bill—one that no one else knew we had. Even the job loss itself ended up being a blessing in the long run—putting us in a position to be ready for a better opportunity that came shortly after. I could share countless times when the encouragement I needed most came at just the right time and in the most unexpected ways.

Moments like these have brought to life Jesus' words to us: *"Consider the ravens: They do not sow or reap, they have no storeroom or barn; yet God feeds them. And how much more valuable you are than birds!"*[13]

Sometimes, the more hopeless our circumstances may seem, the more we become aware of God's provision, comfort, and nearness in ways we never would have looked for or been aware of before. And when we do, our hearts are encouraged to see that God is personal and compassionate. He not only cares about our pain; he wants to show us that he's present in it.

Friend, do you feel hopeless in your circumstances? If you do, I'm so sorry. I can't imagine the pain you must be enduring, but I want to encourage you to not lose hope. May our seemingly hopeless circumstances teach us that we should never put our ultimate hope in better circumstances, because that's never a guarantee. Instead, may our circumstances lead us to Jesus and the hope he gives—a hope that is beyond what this world can offer.

As Betsie ten Boom was carried away to the hospital ward just before she died, she whispered to her sister, *"We must tell people what we have learned here. We must tell them that there is no pit so deep that He is not deeper still. They will listen to us, Corrie, because we have been there."*[14]

If you are feeling hopeless today, be encouraged. In this world, we will have sorrows, but when our life is in God's hands, we are never hopeless. For *"there is no pit so deep that He is not deeper still."*

5

He holds our tears in pain

I am no stranger to pain. Even as I write these words, my body aches within me. As the years go by and chronic pain is a constant, I long for relief. This body often feels more like my enemy than my ally. Of all the difficulties and trials that I've faced, physical pain is often the most relentless and debilitating. Unlike certain forms of pain that we might be able to temporarily distract ourselves from, physical pain demands our attention and impacts nearly every aspect of life. To add insult to injury, our pain is often then multiplied as the chronic nature of it forces us into isolation and silent suffering.

I'll be the first to admit that physical pain can quickly bring us to the end of ourselves. At first, we may persevere with the hope and confidence that answers and healing are just around the corner, just waiting to resume life as normal. But when they aren't, and we watch the life, abilities, and enjoyments we once had fade into the distance, disappointment, grief, despair, hopelessness, and bitterness can quickly seep into our veins. The questions are often not far behind: *what did I do to deserve this? What purpose is there in a life consumed by pain? Is God punishing me for something? What hope do I have if this is the rest of my life?*

If you can relate, I'm so sorry that you're suffering in this way. I don't pretend to know the challenges you face and I certainly don't claim to understand the unique nature or length of your pain. But I do know what it feels like when chronic pain derails plans, or causes you to toss and turn in discomfort, desperate for relief. I do know what it's like to hear a doctor's treatment plan, while deep down wondering if there's any point in even trying anymore. I know what it's like to look fine on the outside while hurting on the inside, carrying a weight that very few can see. And I know what it's like to feel like a disappointment to others, a burden to loved ones, and a problem to be fixed.

There are certainly no simple answers or quick fixes, but over time, I've learned that there is hope to be found even in this place. A hope that has carried me through the darkest days and deepest pain, and which I hope to encourage you with in your own pain as well.

One true remedy

If you've dealt with any form of chronic pain or illness for very long, I'm sure you could share countless experiences of those who have shared dos and don'ts, treatments options, or bullet-proof solutions that healed their Uncle Bob or friend Judy. Although most people have good intentions, without fail those comments always come across as "you just haven't done enough," or "if you just do what I did, things will improve." While we do need to be open and teachable to the wisdom and experiences of others, these solutions are never a guarantee and they always fall short of true comfort. There is only One who knows exactly what we need, when we need it, and how to provide it—God himself.

Hope in anything or anyone else will always fall short. We can and should seek help when and where possible, but our hope can't be in a doctor or treatment—because they're never a guarantee. Our hope can't be in "better days" ahead of us— because that may or may not come in our lifetime. And our hope can't be in our own strength, resources, or wisdom—because we're limited in our understanding and abilities.

But there is a remedy that never fails.

We can bring our pain to the One who created us and knows us better than we know ourselves. And if he created us, certainly he wants what's best for us.

It helps me to think of it this way: in the Bible, God is described as the Potter and we as the clay. The Bible tells us that God carefully and lovingly creates and shapes each of us into form, with unique looks, talents, personalities, and purposes. Whether we know it or not, we all belong to him, the Potter. But after God created the world and us, we rejected him and rebelled against his good plan for us. Since that day, the cracks of sin, pain, suffering, and weakness have entered our lives. We try to mend those cracks with anything we can find, but the defect still remains. For me, I've experienced the cracks made by my sinful choices, but I've also felt the painful cracks of illness and suffering of various kinds, simply from living in this sinful world. I can try to ignore that the cracks are there, or do what I can to fix them, but the reality is that I'm the pot—I simply can't fix myself. Instead, I need to humble myself, admit that I'm broken and cracked, and return to God, my Potter, to be restored as he intended me to be.

As painful and frustrating (perhaps even debilitating) as these cracks may be, we are not hopeless because we still have access to the One who created us and wants to heal us. That doesn't mean he will remove the crack of pain in this life, but when we're restored back to the Potter, he promises full healing will one day come. In the meantime, he also assures us that those cracks won't be wasted and pointless.

Here's where our hope can be found when we don't have the promise of our pain being removed. God, our Potter, tells us that he will use the cracks that seem useless to us for our own good. There's a man in the Bible named Paul, who experienced countless forms of pain. Even after all of his suffering, he confidently wrote, *"We have this treasure in jars of clay to show that this all-surpassing power is from God and not from us. We are hard pressed on every side, but not crushed; perplexed, but not in despair; persecuted, but not abandoned; struck down, but not destroyed."*[15]

Centuries ago, people would use clay pots for many daily purposes, but when a pot would break, they wouldn't throw it away as we might. Strangely enough, they'd use it to hold their most treasured possessions. That way, if thieves broke in, they'd likely ignore the broken and seemingly useless pot, missing the treasure it held inside.

What we see as irreversible weakness and pain, and cracks that render us purposeless, God sees as an opportunity to fill us with his power and strength to shine through those cracks. He gives us not just the privilege of having Jesus' strength in us, but the treasure of his presence to shine through us to others.

Friend, do you feel like your pain is pointless and these cracks have done nothing but break you and take good from you? Be encouraged—God, the Potter, made you with a purpose. This pain and the cracks you long to be free from may be the very thing that God is using to help you see that the realities of sin in the world and our lives are far more devastating than any suffering we might endure. He longs to restore your relationship with him, and to offer you healing and wholeness that will last far beyond this world. Even more, he can use this pain, illness, or suffering in your life to fill you with treasures that only he can give. Doctors may fail you, but God is the great Physician. Friends may not see your pain, but God sees it to the fullest. You may feel useless in your pain, but God can use that pain for purposes that show you and those around you his love, compassion, comfort, and strength.

Practical care in our pain

There are days when even though I believe God loves me and will not waste this pain in my life, the pain screams louder. I admit, there have even been days when life felt too bleak to go on.

But in these moments, I've also seen how practical and close God is to me. He doesn't tell me to toughen up and deal with it; he meets me in practical ways that show he cares about my pain—giving me what I need to endure it.

And I'm not the only one who's experienced this. There's an account in the Bible of a man named Elijah who was exhausted from battle and on the run from his enemies. He was weary and worn out, to the point of despairing of life itself. So when he came to a broom bush, he sat down under it and prayed that he would die. He cried out to God to take his life—he had had enough! Then he lay down under the bush and fell asleep—until an angel touched him and told him to get up and eat. Looking around, he saw bread baked over hot coals, and a jar of water. He ate and drank and went back to sleep. Then an angel of God came back again and said that he should get up and eat because otherwise the journey would be too much for him. So Elijah got up and ate and drank. Strengthened by the food that was miraculously provided by God himself, he traveled on . . . God saw Elijah's exhaustion and despair, and had compassion on him. He didn't tell him to "man up" or give him a spiritual "talking to"; he provided him with food, water, and rest in the middle of the wilderness. God cared about Elijah's practical needs, knowing that he didn't have enough strength to go on. Elijah was honest with God about how he felt, and God responded with compassion, giving him exactly what he needed most to regain perspective and strength.

Friend, the same is true for us. For purposes beyond what we can see, God may not remove our pain, but he gives us compassion and comfort, and promises to provide what we need.

I've experienced this personally. There have been seasons when I felt beaten down and discouraged, only to have someone show up at my door, unannounced, with a lavish dinner that made us feel spoiled. At a time when I felt isolated and convinced no one could see my pain, a friend called just to say they were thinking of me and asked if they could visit to see how I was. And there have even been times when I felt crippled by pain, unsure of how I was going to fulfill a commitment, but then was miraculously pain free for the exact amount of time I needed to accomplish it—with the pain returning shortly after. Then again, at other times, I've still felt the pain, but somehow had the strength to endure it—a strength that was beyond myself.

There's no sugarcoating how life-altering chronic pain can be. And we should always use whatever means God gives us to improve our situation. But whether we find physical relief or not, this truth and hope about God's compassion and provision remains the same.

We may have cracks running through our lives—even some that threaten to break us completely. But these cracks are not meant to destroy us and render us useless. Rather, they are meant to lead us to the One who created us and is the only One who can fully heal, restore, and provide for what we need.

Your painful cracks don't have to have the last word. Bring them to the Potter. For that's where you will find healing for eternity, and strength and rest for today.

6

He holds our tears in waiting

It was eight painstaking months of watching bills pile high and our savings run dry. We waited and waited, seeking every job opportunity that came, only to watch the door slam shut each time.

Three months after my husband had taken a promising job, we were left in shock when we learned the company was letting go of seventy-five percent of its employees—including him. To make matters worse, since he had been hired just three months prior, there would be no severance pay to ease the blow. Shortly after, a pandemic hit and companies ceased hiring.

With seven mouths to feed (including a Chinese exchange student at the time), five of us going through costly Lyme disease treatments, and growing needs, our stress and worry increased by the day.

And the waiting went on—month after month.

I admit, this long season of joblessness was both painful and confusing. We had so much need and so little provision. We stopped our needed medical treatments, said no to activities that our children enjoyed, and swallowed our pride as we survived on food stamps. Although this lengthy season would eventually be used to change the trajectory of our lives for the better, those eight months of waiting were excruciating and difficult to understand.

And I know that we're not alone. Most of life involves some form of waiting. We anxiously wait in traffic when we're running late for an important meeting; time slows as we wait for the dreaded test results; we wait in hope of a broken relationship being restored; a couple waits each month in the hope of a positive pregnancy test; the world waits for the desired return of normalcy after a life-altering pandemic; and the list goes on.

I'll be the first to admit that I don't like to wait. And I'm yet to meet anyone who does! It makes us feel out of control, anxious, impatient, and frustrated. And it's just plain inconvenient.

But could it be that these seasons of waiting are not random or pointless? Could it be that there's a God who's in control and has a purpose in our waiting?

After more seasons of waiting than I can count—both short and long—I'm increasingly confident that he does.

More than that, we can find rest in our waiting.

Our waiting is not a surprise to God

There's an account in the Bible where we see this play out in a way that's been an encouragement to me in the confusion and difficulty of waiting. During Jesus' time on earth, many people came to him for healing, knowing that he had the power of God in him and could heal them in an instant if he chose to do so. When a man named Lazarus, the brother of Martha and Mary, became deathly ill, the two women immediately sent word for Jesus, knowing that he loved Lazarus and had the power to heal him.

But Jesus' response wasn't at all what I expected it to be. The Bible tells us that Jesus loved Martha, Mary, and Lazarus, but that when Jesus heard how sick Lazarus was, he decided to stay where he was for two more days!

He waited. What?!

If Jesus really loved Martha, Mary, and Lazarus, and if he really was in control, why would he delay? And if he really loves you and me, and is in control of everything that happens, why does he allow our painful seasons of waiting—especially when the waiting leads to more pain?

In these moments, we hit a crossroad. We have two choices. We can believe Jesus isn't really God and doesn't have the power that he claims he has. Or we can believe he is God and has purposes beyond what we can see in the moment.

There's a purpose to our waiting

When the two days had passed, Jesus finally told those with him that their friend Lazarus had fallen asleep and he was going there to wake him up. Naturally, those following him were quite perplexed, as I would have been. But it turns out that Jesus was actually talking about Lazarus' death. After Jesus' disciples looked at him in confusion, he plainly told them that Lazarus was dead and that he was glad not to have been there for their sake, so that they might believe.

Jesus didn't arrive until four days after Lazarus had died and been buried. Understandably, Martha and Mary were confused and upset by his delay. Didn't Jesus care? Martha actually said to Jesus that if he had been with them, their brother wouldn't have died. I admit, I've felt that same confusion at times. If God is in control and my life is not just a string of random events, then why did he delay when our family was suffering so greatly? We weren't asking for a mansion by the ocean; we simply wanted the means to provide for food, shelter, and the medical needs of our family. But he still chose to wait. Why?

Maybe, like Jesus' delay in coming to Lazarus, he has something greater in store for us. Maybe he wants to give us peace in knowing there's a purpose in our waiting. Most importantly, maybe he wants it to lead us to search for hope and life in Jesus, rather than putting our hope in what we're waiting for—just as he did for Mary and Martha. Jesus finally explained to Martha, *"I am the resurrection and the life. The one who believes in me will live, even though they die; and whoever lives by believing in me will never die. Do you believe this?"*[16] Martha replied that she did believe Jesus was *"the Messiah, the Son of God"*[17] who had come as promised to save the world. Jesus delayed, but in the waiting, he showed Martha (and everyone around her) that he wanted to do more than save Lazarus from a physical death; he wanted to save each one of them from death beyond this life. If they believed in him to give them life, although they would still die physically in this world, they would be alive with him for eternity.

In our waiting, he's wanting the same for you and me.

He cares about our pain even as we wait

Even if we believe there's good at the end of our waiting, it doesn't take away the difficulty and heartache as we struggle to understand this. That is why I'm comforted by Jesus' response to Mary when she saw him coming. She fell at his feet and, as I mentioned before, said that if he had been there, her brother wouldn't have died. When Jesus saw her weeping, and those around her weeping, he was moved and deeply troubled. So Jesus asked where Lazarus had been laid and they led him to the tomb.

As they did, the Bible says that Jesus wept.

Even though Jesus knew this story would end in miraculous healing, when he saw Mary weeping, it grieved him so deeply that he wept at the sight of her grief.

Friend, this same God sees our tears of grief and weeps with us in the pain of our longing. He knows the end of the story, yet still weeps with us as though our tears are his own.

He wants to show us his power and glory in what seems impossible

I'm so thankful that Lazarus' death and Martha and Mary's grief weren't the end of the story.

When they finally reached the place where Lazarus had been laid, Jesus said to those around him, *"Did I not tell you that if you believe, you will see the glory of God?"*[18] They took away the stone that was laid across the tomb's entrance. Then Jesus called in a loud voice, *"Lazarus, come out!"*[19] Lazarus came out of the tomb with his hands and feet wrapped in linen, and a cloth around his face. Jesus told the people to unwrap his grave clothes and let him go. Jesus chose to wait—not in coldness or indifference, but in love. He was showing them the miraculous power and glory of God through the waiting.

I can now say with confidence that the same has been true for my family.

We have not experienced the excitement of seeing someone raised from the dead. However, our eight months of waiting, with one dead end after another, led to an opportunity that we would've never known to look for. After several miraculous details that couldn't have been orchestrated by anyone but God himself, we uprooted and moved us across the country to a new city, job, and community. They have all been an incredible gift to us in more ways than I can express. If we had had our own way—a quicker and easier way—we would have missed out on something so much greater. But because God's in control, loves us, and knows what's best for us, he delayed. In the end, we saw and believed that there truly is a God that we can trust with every detail of our lives.

Friend, are you in a difficult season of waiting? We don't have a guarantee that the thing we're waiting for will happen as we think it will or want it to, but it might be that God has something better in store for you than you can see right now. Whatever the outcome of your circumstances may be, you can trust that the same God who wept with Mary and breathed life into Lazarus is with you in your waiting.

7

He holds our tears in fear

"Your ankle will continue to worsen the more you use it. Eventually, you'll be unable to walk on it. After five surgeries and multiple attempts, the damage is too great. There's nothing else we can do until you're eligible for an ankle replacement several years down the road."

My mind raced. *No, this isn't possible. There has to be more that can be done. I'm only thirty-five and have four little kids to care for!* As soon as the doctor's words and my reality began to fully sink in, fear began to rise. *How will I care for my family if I can't walk? Will I always have to face the disappointment in my children's eyes when I say that I can't go for a walk or play soccer in the yard?* Between slowly losing my ability to walk, the unknown future of my chronic illness, the worries over the trajectory of our son's struggles, and the finances that were quickly draining, fear of the future had a death grip around my neck.

Regardless of how much I tried to convince myself that it would somehow all be okay (after all, they say where there's a will, there's a way, right?), deep down I knew that I didn't have that guarantee. How could I not fear when I knew my fears would most likely become a reality?

Maybe you're wondering the same. Maybe the pain and suffering that you're facing have brought fresh fears, anxieties, and unknowns: *where can I find peace in a world where there is so much to fear and circumstances that paralyze me with worry?* Cancer strikes people who seem to be the beacon of health; car accidents happen in a split second; parents bury children; stock markets crash; finances run dry; burglars break in; tornadoes strike; and wars break out. The list of things to fear is endless.

But we have a choice. You and I can respond to our fears in one of two ways. We can live our life with a white-knuckled grip on everything that we're afraid of losing and live in fear over every "what if?" Or we can learn to accept that we aren't in control and look for comfort and peace outside of ourselves.

You see, fear isn't always bad. At times, it alerts us to a very real danger, causing us to run to safety or call for help. In the same way, the fears we face can alert us to the fact that something fundamental isn't right. We aren't meant to be on our own, trying to rule our own lives. We are meant to live in the safety, protection, and care of the God who created us, trusting our lives in his hands, instead of our own.

The Bible tells us that the God who made the whole world and rules over the heavens and earth doesn't need us to serve or give him anything. But he has given life and breath to everyone and everything. He made all mankind from one man (Adam) in order to fill the earth. He has appointed every moment in history and has placed each of us where we are for a specific time and purpose. He did all of this so that we will seek him, reach out to him, and find him, even though he's never far from us. He's always close, but our eyes need to be opened to see we need him because we were made to know him.

So when fear begins to creep into my heart again, it reminds me that I need to stop focusing on what I can't control. Instead, I need to find comfort in the fact that there's a God who's not only in control of all things, but who sees me personally and loves me. He knows what's best for me and can bring it about—even if that comes through allowing the very thing I may fear. He tells us that he knows the plans that he has for us—not for our harm, but for our good, to give us a future and a hope.

Friend, the events of your life and my life are not random. We are not simply at the mercy of chance, fate, or karma. If we were, we'd have everything to fear, always peering around the corner in terror of what might be lying in wait. Or on the flipside, we might meticulously try to control every single moment of our lives in the hope that we might somehow keep ourselves from the pain of this world. That's exhausting, isn't it?

But, thankfully, there is a God. And he is in complete control of every atom, molecule, minute, and circumstance of our lives. We are not at the mercy of shifting winds because there is a God who rules over the wind, even when it may appear chaotic and out of control.

However, knowing that there's a God who's in control is only part of our comfort. We've all known someone who's used their position of control at the expense of others and for their own personal gain. That's why it's equally important to know that God is good. His nature, his character, his very being is good, kind, compassionate, just, and trustworthy. The Bible says that we can cast our anxieties and fears on him because he cares for us. But telling our fears and anxieties to someone is only comforting if we believe they have our best in mind and have the power to do something about it. So God assures those who put their trust in him, *"So do not fear, for I am with you; do not be dismayed, for I am your God. I will strengthen you and help you, I will uphold you with my righteous right hand."*[20]

When I start to fear what life might be like as my ankle worsens, I don't have to let the fear grip my heart. I can be honest with God about the things I fear. At the same time, when I remember and believe that he knows what's best for me, I can trust that he will either heal me or provide what I need.

When bad things happen to good people

We've all wondered from time to time, *if there's a God who's in control and wants what's best for us, why does he let bad things happen to anyone, let alone those who trust and follow him?*

Well, it wasn't always this way.

At the beginning of time, God created a perfect world. There was no evil, pain, suffering, or death. Adam and Eve, the first two people on the face of earth, were made in God's image. He walked, talked, and enjoyed a perfect relationship with them. Life was exactly what we all long for it to be: safe, peaceful, beautiful, perfect, and free from sin, suffering, and death. But Adam and Eve chose to disobey the one command God had given them for their own protection: not to eat from the tree of the knowledge of good and evil. Since then, every part of this world has been affected by the curse of sin, the result of rejecting the God who created us to know, trust, and obey him. Our pain is simply the consequences of living in a world that has rejected the God who created it. But even before God created the world or sin entered it, God had a plan to use our rebellion for his good purposes and to restore us to a relationship with him.

Remarkably, he still grieves the pain that sin has brought into our lives. Despite the fact that we've rejected him, he still loves us, pursues us, grieves with us, and remains good in all he does.

Joni Eareckson Tada, a remarkable woman who became a quadriplegic from a diving accident at the age of seventeen, explained it well in her book *When God Weeps*. She wrote,

When people sin against us they alone bear the responsibility, and God will one day judge them. When hurricanes strike, it's not irreligious for the National Hurricane Center to give a scientific explanation. When disease stalks, there's a traceable medical reason. When animals cause problems, they're acting on instinct. When accidents happen, it's okay to call them accidents—even the Bible does. When babies die and whole populations starve and cocaine junkies blow away frightened convenience-store clerks, God weeps for his world. All these things are true. But the Bible insists on another truth simultaneously. All during these sins, typhoons, illnesses, mishaps, snake bites, crib deaths, famines, and gas-station robberies—God hasn't taken his hand off the wheel for thirty seconds. His plans are being accomplished despite, yes, even through, these tragedies. They are tragedies. He considers them so. He loathes the wickedness and misery and destruction itself—but he has determined to steer what he hates to accomplish what he loves.[21]

Friend, I've had countless things to fear in my life—many of which have come true. I planned on playing collegiate sports, but a freak accident left me with an injury that would change the trajectory of the rest of my life. God hates the pain that loss brought into my life, but he used that redirection to lead me to the man that I married, the children we now have, and opportunities that I never would have pursued otherwise. It's as if God was saying to me in my fears, "Sarah, I grieve with you over this loss and my heart aches with you in your pain, but I am with you and can see things that you aren't yet able to see. All you feel right now is the pain and fear of the future, but I have a good plan for you that you will one day see as you trust and follow me."

We won't always understand why God allows certain things to happen, and there are tragedies that occur because we live in a broken world. But we don't have to live in fear when we believe that God's in control, knows what's best for us, and can work through our trials for our good and to help us know him more.

He holds our tears in fear

You may have a lot to fear right now. But God—
who created you, knows you, and loves you—says
with the compassion of a Father, *"Come to me, all you
who are weary and burdened, and I will give you rest."*[22]

8

He holds our tears in shame

I squeezed my eyes shut, desperately hoping to awake from this nightmare. But a knock at the door jolted me into reality. This was a nightmare, but one I was very much living.

The nurse entered my room, checked to make sure I hadn't harmed myself, and left as quickly as she came. Staring at this room's four white walls, it felt as empty as I did. *How did I get here?* I sighed under my breath.

I was seventeen. I was hurting and angry as I watched my life crumble before my eyes. Sitting here in the barren room of the adolescent psychiatric ward, I was left with nothing but the pain of what I'd lost and the shame that I'd gained.

Why me? After pouring ten years of my life into the pursuit of collegiate basketball, why did I have to lose it all at the hands of an abusive coach and life-altering injury? Why was I chronically sick while those around me went on with life as normal? And why, on top of all that I've already lost, did I have to experience the shame of sexual abuse and harassment at the hands of my peers?

If there's a good and loving God, why would he allow so much pain if he could have stopped it?

I needed answers. I believed there was a God and had been told that he was good and loving—so much that he sent his own Son, Jesus, to die on a cross so that I could be forgiven and accepted. But if he was good and loved me enough to die for me, why didn't he protect me from the pain of this world?

As I wrestled with my thoughts and questions, a familiar story came to mind. A story that Jesus told in the Bible about a Father and his two sons. A day came when the younger son decided that he wanted more than what he had under the protection and provision of his father—he wanted the thrill of what might be and the taste of freedom. So he came up with a plan. He asked his father for his inheritance, to which his father obliged, splitting the inheritance equally between his two sons.

In the excitement of his new-found freedom, the younger son set out to experience the pleasures of the world around him. Before long, he had carelessly used all he had and was faced with the sober reality of being alone and penniless as famine spread across the land. In desperation, he took the only job he could find—feeding and living among the pigs of a farmer.

Needless to say, he had hit rock bottom.

Coming home

I, too, knew what it was like to hit rock bottom. *Am I that prodigal child?* I wondered. The Bible says that God, my Heavenly Father, created me to know him and live in the safety, protection, and provision of being his child. But in my desire for independence and freedom, I had been searching for happiness, contentment, purpose, and value in anything but following him. Although many of those things satisfied for a time, they always led to a familiar sting of disappointment and the ache of emptiness.

Maybe I've been asking the wrong question all along. Instead of questioning, *why would a good God let bad things happen?* maybe I should be asking, *why should I expect good from the God who I've run from?* You see, the prodigal son wasn't facing pain because the father was punishing him; his suffering was merely the natural consequences of looking elsewhere for what he'd had all along with his father. The goodness of the father hadn't changed; the heart of the son had.

The same was true for me. I had chosen to live my own way. So I was experiencing the pain of living in a world that has walked away from the God who created us to know, trust, and follow him. I wasn't only wanting to have my own way; I was blaming God for the consequences that naturally came because of it.

But, thankfully, that wasn't the end of the story—for me or the younger brother.

The young son eventually saw his foolishness and longed to be back in the provision and care of his father. So he set off for home with his head bowed in shame. He knew he didn't deserve anything from his father, but he hoped that if he sought his father's forgiveness, maybe he'd be received back as one of his lowly hired servants.

As the son neared his home, his father saw him from far away and was filled with compassion for him. His father immediately ran to his son, threw his arms around him and kissed him as though he'd been waiting for this day since the moment he watched his son walk away. The son knew he didn't deserve this kind of greeting, so he humbly confessed that he had sinned against God and him, and knew that he no longer deserved to be called a son.

To the son's shock, his dad yelled to his servants to grab the best robe, ring, and sandals to lavish on his son. Even more, he called for a feast to celebrate his return, saying, *"For this son of mine was dead and is alive again; he was lost and is found."*[23] This was an occasion to celebrate!

As I read this story, tears began to roll down my face. I was experiencing the pain of my own sin, the sin of others, and the suffering that comes from living in a world that's rejected its Creator. But God wasn't punishing me or looking at me in anger and disappointment. He was looking at me with the eyes of a compassionate and loving Father, ready to receive me with open arms and rejoice at my return.

What shame tells us

What do you imagine the son felt as he sat among the pigs? Regret? Embarrassment? Shame?

Probably all of the above.

Whether we recognize it or not, we all know the feeling of shame. We feel embarrassed when our imperfections are exposed. We feel guilty when we know that something is wrong, but do it anyway. We feel shame when someone violates or takes advantage of us, condemning ourselves for allowing it to happen. We feel insecure when deep down we know that we're vulnerable to our own weaknesses and lack of control in life. But underneath it all, the feeling of shame stems from the realization that we can't live up to God's perfect standards. We may call them "mistakes, slip ups, or weakness," but, in reality, they're sin—disobedience to God's commands. Mistakenly thinking that if we just do enough good, God will accept us and we'll feel worthy of being accepted, we exhaust ourselves with our efforts.

But that feeling of shame and guilt is not meant to crush us; it's meant to open our eyes to the true state of our hearts, like the foolishness of the younger brother did. We have two choices. We can either sit in our shame (like that son who sat in the filth of pigs), or we can run to the Father, ask for his forgiveness, and be received in the goodness and love of his open arms.

So does that mean that God will protect us from pain and heartache?

At times, yes—maybe even in ways we'll never know. But often, no. As long as we live in this world, we will inevitably experience the pain, struggles, disappointments, losses, and heartache that touch everyone and everything that has breath.

Even the younger son's return to his father didn't exempt him from future pain. He could still get sick, break an arm, lose a loved one, and face the effects of aging. Similarly, my forgiveness and restored relationship to God doesn't mean I'm exempt from a severe ankle injury, a child with special needs, seasons of financial struggle, being hurt by others, or loved ones dying. And it doesn't mean that I'm exempt from having to face the natural consequences of some of my own choices. But it does mean that God will be with me through it all. He will provide the comfort and strength that I need in it. And he won't waste the pain that apart from him would gain me nothing. The Bible says that *in all things God works for the good of those who love him, who have been called according to his purpose.*[24] He may allow suffering, but because he rules over it, he can use it to accomplish his good purposes—even if we can't see or understand those purposes in the moment.

I learned the hard way that we were never meant to live independently from God, our Heavenly Father. I've had to face the shame and painful results of my choices. But in God's love for me, he showed me that there's a better way. We can stop choosing to live our own way or trying to earn God's favor. Instead, we can humbly ask for his forgiveness, which Jesus bought for us through his death on a cross. He then rose back to life to defeat death. When we come to God, he will rejoice and welcome us with open arms. He will remove our shame and give us Jesus' perfect record of righteousness in its place. With our guilt removed, we find peace with God and receive eternal life with him.

As I've experienced since that painful but life-changing time in the hospital, trials will still come, losses will still cause grief, and physical death will still one day come. But you and I can trust that he is a good Father who loves us and knows what's best for us. When we are safe in his care, we may experience the pain of this world. However, we will also experience his peace in our fears, comfort in our heartache, joy in our sorrow, strength in our weakness, and hope in hopelessness. He promises *"that neither death nor life, neither angels nor demons, neither the present nor the future, nor any powers, neither height nor depth, nor anything else in all creation, will be able to separate us from the love of God that is in Christ Jesus our Lord."*[25]

Friend, whether you're weighed down in shame, grieving a loss, or feeling the emptiness and fragility of everything around you, know that you have a Heavenly Father who longs to receive you with the joy of a Father whose prodigal child has returned. Come to him and you will find freedom from your shame, comfort in your grief, and a satisfaction and security that nothing in this world can give. He will rejoice over you, saying, *"For this son [or daughter] of mine was dead and is alive again; he [or she] was lost and is found."*

That is worth celebrating.

9

He remembers those in his book

The room was quiet and sterile as the nurses shuffled around to each patient, attending to their IVs and patiently listening to their discomforts, questions, and concerns. The smell of alcohol and bleach wafted through the air as I sat and stared at each drop of blood that dripped with perfect precision into my IV line. Drip. Drip. Drip. Time seemed to slow as I watched each drop travel through the PICC (peripherally inserted central catheter) line, returning my pint of blood now mixed with a medicine that would go to battle against the infections that ravaged my body.

Every day for nine weeks, I returned to this chair for blood to be drawn, treated, and infused back into my veins. I would try to pass the time with the patients around me, sharing our health struggles, swapping treatment tips, and discussing the questions and struggles we wrestled with as we fought to live the life our bodies kept us from living.

One day, a conversation arose about the purpose of our pain and where we could find comfort and hope. One person shared how weary she was and wondered what the point of living was if she would suffer for the rest of her life. Another person shared with confidence that they believed God would heal them no matter what. And one shared how her illness had caused her to think more about the fact that she would one day breathe her last and, in all honesty, she was afraid of not knowing what she'd be met with, if anything.

As I listened to the conversation and added a few thoughts, I started feeling woozy and laid back in my chair. My thoughts drifted off as I went back to watching the familiar drip of the IV. *Why does God sometimes not heal us if he loves us so much?* I wondered. *The Bible says that Jesus came to heal the sick and open the eyes of the blind, so why had he not healed me, my son, and my other children? What hope do I have in a life filled with pain and sorrow?*

Suddenly, a thought struck me: maybe my physical illness isn't my greatest problem. Just as I needed something outside of myself to heal my body, maybe I needed a Savior outside of myself to save my soul.

The truth is, we are all sick. Not necessarily physically, but spiritually. However, it wasn't always that way.

As I shared earlier, God created the first man and woman (Adam and Eve) in his image and without sin. As hard as it is to imagine, they lived in a perfect world, physically walked with God himself, and had nothing to fear. But because God created human beings with free will, they had a choice. They could choose to trust and obey him. Or they could break their perfect relationship by disobeying the one command he'd given for their own protection: not to eat from one tree, the tree of the knowledge of good and evil. Sadly, they believed the lie that God was withholding something good from them, disobeyed, and ate from the tree, bringing sin into the world and into every human being from that day on. The perfect relationship with God was broken, and sin, pain, suffering, and death became our reality. We ruined God's perfect world and broke the heart of the One who made us.

At this point, we can feel hopeless. We live in a painful world, our hearts are naturally bent to love ourselves and hate God, and deep down, if we're honest, we all know that we can't change ourselves. No matter how much I try to do what's right and convince myself that I'm naturally a "good person," pride, selfishness, bitterness, laziness, jealousy, and so on quickly remind me that I still fall short of God's perfect standards.

But here's the good news; here's the greatest reason we can know that God truly does love us so much that he cares about our pain, loneliness, sorrow, fears, grief, shame, and tears. Even though we are all born into sin and are enemies of God because of it, God loved us so much that he sent his Son Jesus to earth as a baby. Jesus was both fully God and fully man. He lived a perfect life that we can't possibly live on our own, and died the death that you and I deserve, taking the punishment for all our sins onto himself. We rejected him. But Jesus loved us so much that he gave his own life in our place so that we can be in relationship with God again. We can't earn God's favor; there is no other way to be forgiven apart from accepting the gift of forgiveness through Jesus. Salvation is only found in Jesus. Like the bag of blood that is cleansed and put back into my body, Jesus gave his own blood to heal ours.

Friend, whether we like to think about it or not, when you and I breathe our last, we will stand before God and face an eternal judgment for the life we've lived on earth. If we have persisted in choosing our own way, refusing to ask for forgiveness and trust Jesus as our Savior, we will receive the punishment that our rejection of God deserves: we will be separated from him for all eternity. But the Bible says, *"If we confess our sins, he is faithful and just and will forgive us our sins and purify us from all unrighteousness."*[26] If we put our trust in Jesus as our Savior and Lord, we no longer have any reason to fear death. Instead of death being our enemy, it's merely the path that leads us to eternal life with Jesus in a new and perfect world. There God says that *"He will wipe every tear from their eyes. There will be no more death or mourning or crying or pain, for the old order of things has passed away."*[27]

Tears and Tossings

Here is where all our tears are meant to lead us—to the One who experienced a greater loneliness, fear, pain, loss, sorrow, weakness, rejection, and shame than any of us ever will. He weeps with us and comforts us in our deepest pain because he's already walked the path of pain in our place. These words, then, become true of us when we accept his gift of forgiveness:

> *You have kept count of my tossings;*
> *put my tears in your bottle.*
> *Are they not in your book?*[28]

Not only do we have hope for eternity, but we have hope for today.

If this life is all there is, then our pain and tears gain us nothing. But if there is a life beyond this, then God, in his love, may allow us to experience the temporary pain of this world with the purpose of it leading us to a healing that will last forever. Even more, our suffering and tears are remembered in his "book" (the same book that the Bible says contains the names of every follower of Jesus). That gives our tears meaning and purpose, and the promise that God will not waste our pain. We can know beyond a doubt that God is for us.

We have a choice

I've said before that I never would have chosen the path that God has allowed me to travel—one with so much pain and loss. But when I see glimpses of what God has done in my life through it, I wouldn't choose any other path.

Now, as I watch each drip of blood that steadily flows back into my veins, I can know that my greatest hope is not found in the chance that this treatment might heal my body and restore the life I desire. If God chooses to, he can heal me in an instant. Instead, my hope is found in the truth that Jesus gave his blood for me, not to temporarily restore my physical health, but to rescue me from my sins and give me life with him forever. I am confident that God can heal me and bring relief to every other trial that I face. However, if he chooses not to, I know that it is because he has something greater to give me in its place— something that will last far beyond earthly relief. And in the meantime, he is drawing near to me, grieving my pain as if it's his own, and comforting me as One who knows the depths of sorrow more than anyone else.

Friend, the same can be true for you.

Whatever you may be facing right now and whatever fears, insecurities, grief, or shame you may be carrying, there is a God who knows and loves you so much. He knows the number of hairs on your head, keeps count of your tossings, and holds every tear that you shed. He is not a distant, angry God who waves a displeased finger at you. He is not indifferent to your pain. He longs for you to put your trust in Jesus as your Savior and receive his forgiveness. And Jesus longs to come near to you, grieve with you, comfort you, strengthen you, grow you, and use every ounce of your sorrow to give you a hope, peace, and joy that this world cannot give.

So come to Jesus, and receive the comfort and hope that he offers you today. You are not alone. Know that there's a God who loves you, knows you, and not only sees your sorrows and tears, but holds them as if they are his own.

Suffering is real. But so is hope.

Notes

2. *He holds our tears in loneliness*

1. Psalm 56:8–9, ESV.
2. Genesis 16:13, ESV.
3. Proverbs 18:24.
4. Deuteronomy 31:8.

3. *He holds our tears in grief and loss*

5. John 14:1–4.
6. John 14:6.
7. Psalm 31:9–10.
8. Isaiah 53:3.
9. Isaiah 53:5.

4. *He holds our tears in hopelessness*

10. Corrie ten Boom, *The Hiding Place* (Hodder & Stoughton, 2004).
11. Psalm 34:18.
12. Corrie ten Boom, *The Hiding Place* (Hodder & Stoughton, 2004).

13. Luke 12:24.
14. Corrie ten Boom, *The Hiding Place* (Hodder & Stoughton, 2004).

5. *He holds our tears in pain*

15. 2 Corinthians 4:7-9.

6. *He holds our tears in waiting*

16. John 11:25-26.
17. John 11:27.
18. John 11:40.
19. John 11:43.

7. *He holds our tears in fear*

20. Isaiah 41:10
21. Joni Eareckson Tada and Steve Estes, *When God Weeps: Why Our Suffering Matters to the Almighty* (Zondervan, first published 1997).
22. Matthew 11:28.

8. *He holds our tears in shame*

23. Luke 15:24.
24. Romans 8:28.
25. Romans 8:37–39.

9. *He remembers those in his book*

26. 1 John 1:9.
27. Revelation 21:4.
28. Psalm 56:8–9, esv.

10Publishing is the publishing house of **10ofThose**.
It is committed to producing quality Christian
resources that are biblical and accessible.

www.10ofthose.com is our online retail arm selling
thousands of quality books at discounted prices.

For information contact: **info@10ofthose.com**
or check out our website: **www.10ofthose.com**